Island Style

by Dennis Long

The Bess Press
P. O. Box 22388
Honolulu, HI 96823

Long, Dennis
   Island Style
Honolulu, Hawaii: The Bess Press, Inc.
128 pages

ISBN: 1-880188-22-8
Copyright © 1992 by The Bess Press, Inc.
ALL RIGHTS RESERVED
Printed in the United States of America

Table of Contents

A is for Aloha Shirt   2
Party My House!   4
Sweet 'n' Sour Pork   6
Wake Up, Hawaii   8
Go Man-go!   10
Hot Summer Night . . . Termite Swarm   12
Sumo Tofu   14
Malihini Manini   16
UH Football Tailgators   18
Hawaiian Rainbow Shave Ice   20
Chili Pepper Water   22
Yaku, I Win   24
Kau Kau   26
Pau Kau Kau   28
Pork Over the Pali   30
Won Ton (W)rappers   32
Good Luck Parade   34
Steamed Mullet   36
No Mo Toy   38
Monster Surf   40
Tutu Hot   42
Shark's Fin Soup   44
Mynah League Baseball   46
Cool Cat   48
Lounge Lizards   50
Chow Fun   52
Fishcake   54

Mount Musubi 56	Steamed Buns 90
Portuguese Man O' War 58	Punahou Carnival 92
Do the Loco Moco 60	Squid Luau 94
Ready . . . Set . . . Bento! 62	I'm in a Pickle 96
Cockfight 64	Leapin' Lizards 98
Local Rock Group 66	Sushi à la Carte 100
Raiders of the Lost Pork 68	Animal Crackahs 102
Peeking Duck . . . Pressed Duck 70	Tako Taco 104
Kumu Hula 72	Flying Fish 106
New Squids on the Block 74	Guava Jam and Pickled Mango 108
Where's Kimo? 76	Banzai Pipeline 110
Pray for Surf! 78	Lunch Wagon . . . Meal on Wheels 112
Mom 'n' Pop Store 80	Oxtail Soup 114
Huli Chicken 82	Local Treats . . . Some Ono! 116
Havin' a Beachin' Day 84	Waikiki Beachboys 118
Kamaboko Slippers 86	The Sandwich Islands 120
Graduation Day . . . Pile on da Leis 88	

Island Style

A is for aloha shirt, we wear each day,
B is for boogie board, we take to play.
Y is for yummy shave ice to eat,
Z is for zori, worn on luau feet.

From ABC to XYZ,
Our alphabet's unique. Agree?

"A" IS FOR ALOHA SHIRT..

Party my house! Starts at four!
Leave your slippers at the door.
Auntie Momi's got her uke,
Uncle Byron's bringing jook.

Maile from Maui's got the poki,
Sashimi, compliments of cousin Moki.
Slippers and shoes are piling high.
Hope to see you here, bumbye.

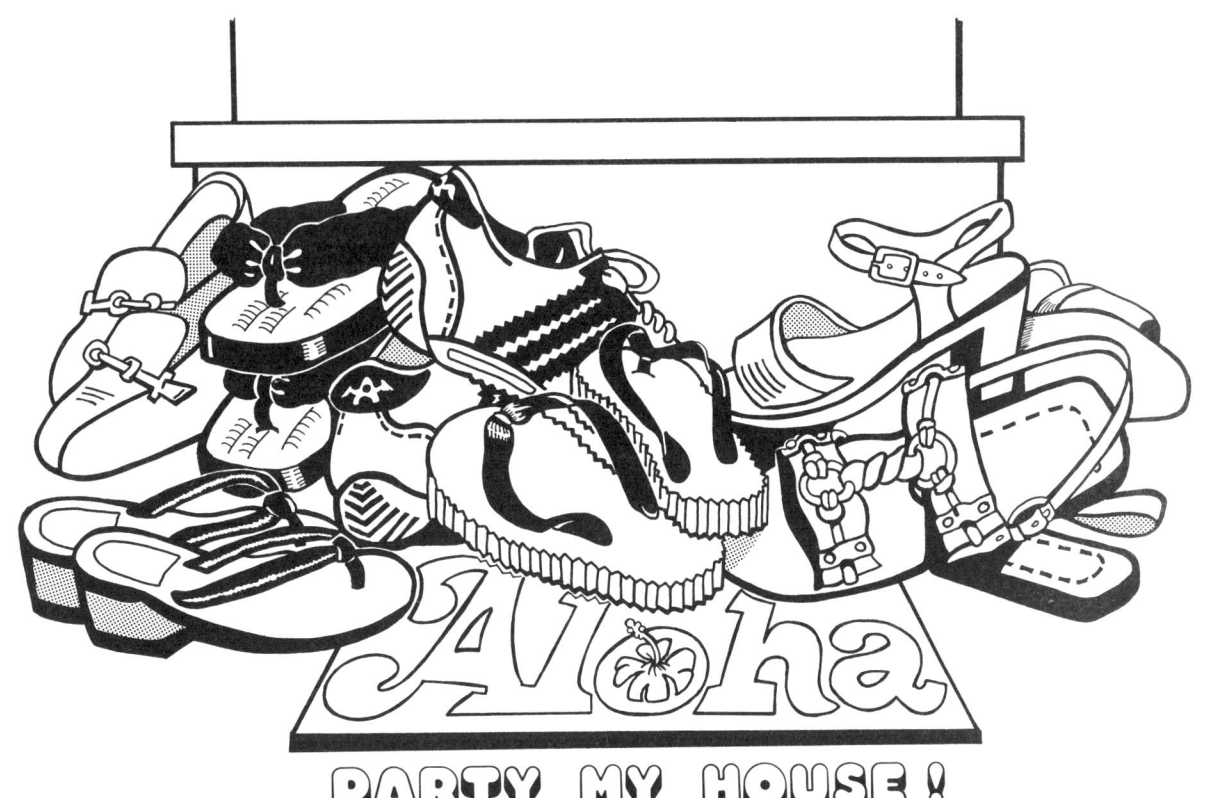

Some like it sweet,
Some like it sour.
It's my favorite Chinese dish
At the lunch hour.
Pig out!

A tranquil sleep;
A peaceful dream;
  Screeeech!
Shattered by a thunderous racket.
  Crash! Bang!
What's that noise?
  Thunk! Thunk!
It's only 6 a.m.!
  Clang! Wham! Clang!
Oh, I forgot. . . . It's trash day.
  Urrroooomm!

It's mango season!
Those sweet, stringy treats
Fall from fruit-laden trees
Into the streets.

The overripe ones . . .
Don't step on those.
They stick to your slippers
And your toes.

Humid summer night.
Termite horde takes flight.
The air still and warm.
Legions will swarm.

They attack without warning.
All gone by next morning.
Not a termite you'll find.
A million wings left behind.

Looming large, stout and white;
Made for hefty appetite.
Tofu's solid, yet it wiggles,
Like sumo stomach . . . firm, yet jiggles.

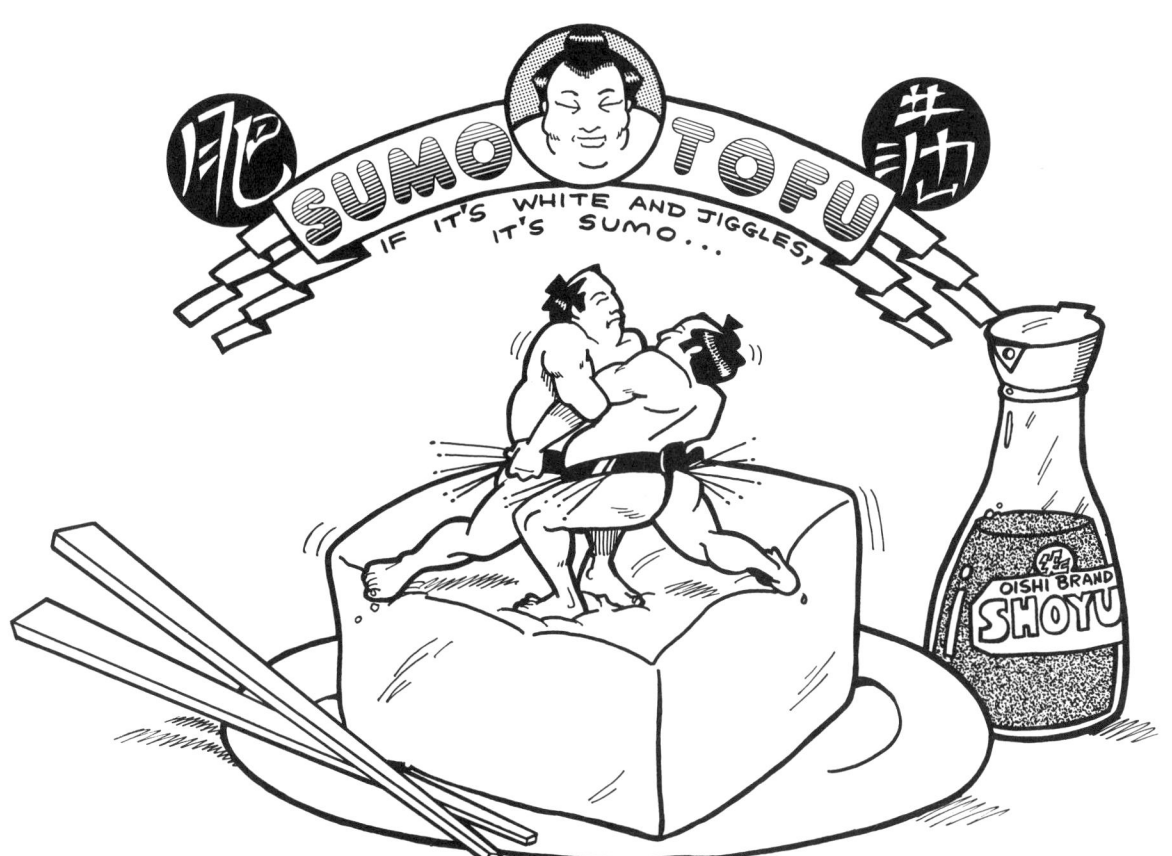

The malihini, or newcomer, is easy to spot.
Shopping bag in hand, takes pictures a lot.
With their pearly-white skin, they're easy shark bait,
For the hungry reef shark who lies in wait.

MALIHINI MANINI

It's Saturday. . . . 'Bows play tonight!
But long before the team's in sight,
The local fans arrive in droves,
And fire up their butane stoves.

Halawa's sky begins to fill
With smoke from a thousand hibachi grills.
Ah! . . . belly's filled . . . so glad we came.
Wait! Almost forgot about the game!

UH FOOTBALL TAILGATORS

The rainbow's colors, frozen in time,
Strawberry, pineapple, lemon-lime.
Want grape, or orange, or root beer? We got 'em!
Or try some azuki beans on the bottom.
Flavors single or mixed is okay.
Shave ice . . .
The coolest treat on a hot summer's day.

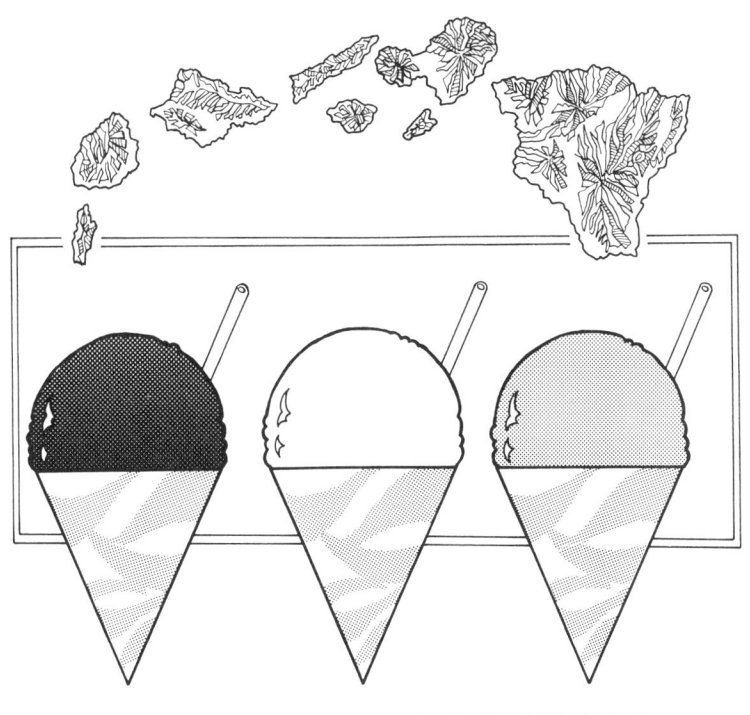

To spice up the laulau you're planning to eat,
Just add a dash of this liquid heat.
Small chili peppers trapped in a bottle
Have the volcano goddess's power at full throttle.

Hanafuda . . . a game of both chance and skill,
A card game that tests Oriental will.
The score tied at midnight,
The full moon I choose,
Gives me bonus points.
I win! You lose!

We're going out to eat!
I've got a hunch
Dad's taking us to get plate lunch!
Chicken? Beef? Pork? It's so hard to choose.
Whatever we pick, we no can lose!

My belt going pop; I overate!
Burp!
Tomorrow, I try the beef-stew plate!

On Old Pali Road, when it gets late,
    You're tempting fate
    If there's bacon on your plate!

With fresh laulau in your truck,
    If you get stuck,
    You're outta luck!

Your engine stalls, while hungry ghosts
Search back seats for a spare pork roast.

Just dump the pig, while making track
To downtown; and don't dare look back!

Place pork filling on top of the skin!
Fold ends over to wrap it in!
Twist the corners and press to seal!
Deep fry the won ton for one heck of a meal!

Lee see as far as the eye can see,
Good fortune cookie smiles down on me.

Maneki neko, daruma doll,
Guarantee success for all.

Lucky symbols; we've got it made.
No storm clouds over this parade.

Those moke mullets!

They make their home on our range.
Their manners are strange.
They play music too loud.
They're one smelly crowd.

A brisk boiling pot
Makes their tempers grow hot.
Don't get them steamed,
Or else you'll be creamed.

No Mo Toy haiku:

> Small kid time; two treats.
> Rice candy and toys inside.
> Now only stickers.

Winter . . . North Shore . . . Monster surf!
Gigantic wave sets pound the turf.
Sunset Beach and Waimea,
Chun's Reef and Pupukea.

Broken boards and shredded fins.
Mother Nature usually wins.

Surfing diehards, foolish and brave,
Hoping for the ultimate wave.
Risking life and limb . . . no fear!
They'll be back, same time next year.

Hot summer day in Haleiwa,
The midday sun gives tutu fever.
It's ninety degrees in the shade!
Break out the ice and lemonade!

It's too, too hot!
Perspiration's dripping;
Off with the muumuus,
We go skinnydipping!

Dorsal fins circling in my dish!
I wish, instead, I'd ordered fish.
Shark's fin soup . . . the soup with a bite.
I should have eaten at home tonight!

Popcorn, peanuts, birdseed!
Nothing could be finer,
Than baseball with the mynahs.
Birds of a feather,
Playing ball together.

Spectators gawking,
Managers squawking.
Strike-outs and fly balls,
Referee's birdcalls.
Pennant fever's running high,
Just don't look up as they fly by!

He's one cool dude, this good-luck feline.
You'll find him at the Banzai Pipeline.
When he goes surfing, things start jumpin'.
The waves are twenty feet and pumpin'!

It's pau hana time; it's after five.
The smoke-filled joints come alive.
As the sun beneath the horizon slips,
Local lounge lizards head down the strip.

They drive to town from miles around,
To hear that karaoke sound.
They're wined and dined all night long,
By Kim and Brandy, Jade and Yong.

Kal bi beef, kim chee, mondoo,
"Buy me drink . . . I sit by you."
The partying won't end 'til dawn,
A dollar earned . . . a dollar gone!

Chow fun, e-min, look fun plate,
Never knew eating could be this great.
Ton fun, won ton pi, gau gee min,
Pull up a plate and dig right in.

I'm taking my girlfriend out for noodles today,
And she'll have fun, fun, fun,
'Til her daddy takes her chopsticks away.

Kamaboko with fins, tail and face,
Come swimming past the marketplace.
Tonight this school of pink and white fish
Will be part of someone's saimin dish.

The Koolau mountains that reach the sky
Are merely mounds of rice piled high
By elves who labor night and day
To get the rice to stick that way.

Like the famed Armada of Spain,
Here comes the Flotilla of Pain!
With the tide, they slowly surround you,
To try to wrap their stingers around you.

Ahoy, the fleet's in!
Better get your feets in!

PORTUGUESE MAN O' WAR

Everybody's doing a brand new dance, now.
Come on, baby, do the Loco Moco.
A favorite dish at breakfast time, if you get the notion.
Come on, baby, do the Loco Moco.

Take two scoops of boiled rice and add a beef patty,
Cover them with fried eggs and top it with gravy.
So come on, come on,
Do the Loco Moco with me!

Get ready with da chopsticks,
All set to grind.
Dig into da bento,
Teriyaki on my mind!

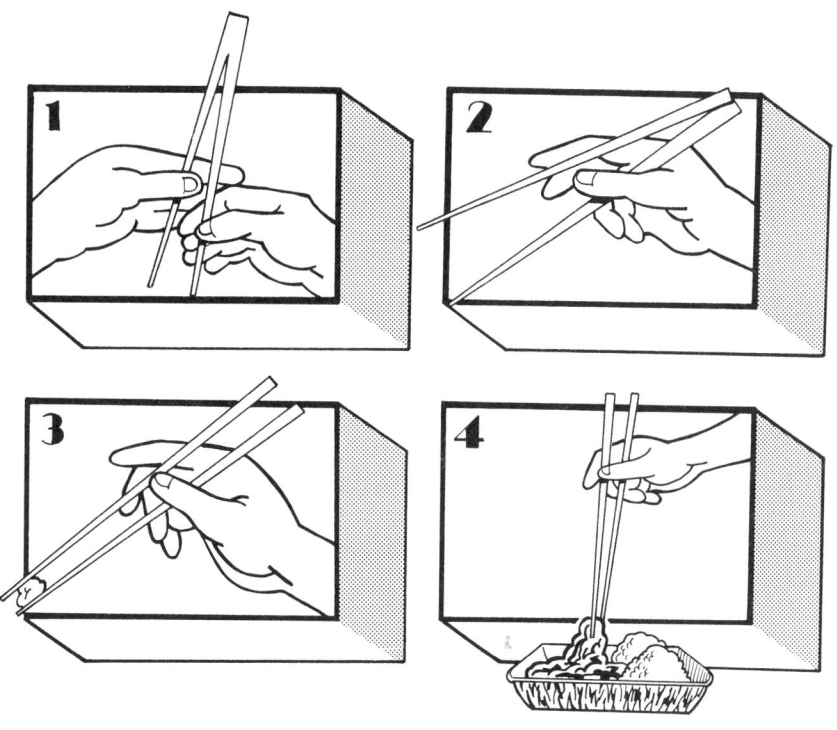

In backwoods Waipahu, the bantamweights box.
The spectators bet on their favorite cocks.
A flurry of feathers; then emerges a winner.
The loser ends up as somebody's dinner.

What's that sound from yonder bay?
The opihi rock band starts to play.

Can you believe, from tiny shells,
The din of ninety decibels?

The wildest gig I ever saw!
I picked them; then I ate them raw!

The lights go out,
The night is black.
The roach marauders
Are on attack.

A thousand feet begin to scurry.
Target: leftover rice and spilled beef curry.
Objective: cracker crumbs and jelly roll.
Mission accomplished: by the Midnight Patrol.
Field of action: the kitchen floor.
Did I just hear the icebox door?

Hey, what you peeking at my friend?
Keep your eyes off her rear end!
Here's a treat you never planned,
Just try it buried in the sand!

In the deep waters of the ocean,
Seaweed skirts are set in motion.

To kumu hula's chants and songs,
We dance and practice all day long.

Our school of fish, comprising ahi,
Ulua, weke, and mahimahi.

We dance with love and dedication,
To meles passed down generations.

We learn to perform in ancient tradition,
While the other ones have all gone fishin'.

The new sensation to hit the isle,
Five cute squids with great vocal style.
From all around, girls push and shove,
To glimpse the faces only mother squids could love.
Come see their show before it's pau.
Tonight they'll end up as squid luau!

Help find Kimo; he's lost, you see,
In the concrete jungle of Waikiki.
His favorite surf spot's taken o'er,
And now abounds with tourists galore.

A slick of sunscreen and tanning lotion,
Now coats the once Pacific Ocean.
Plumeria trees and mynahs choke,
From thick tour bus and moped smoke.

The restless natives in the know,
Left this place long ago.
But stubborn Kimo's hard to teach.
He'll stay until he finds the beach.

Pray for surf! We might as well;
The horizon's flat, without a swell.
We planned a day of shooting the curls;
Oh, well . . .
At least on the beach, we can check out the girls!

After-school snacks . . . today's the day!
We're buying manapua and ginger senbei.
Rock salt plum and li hing mui,
Shredded mango and something gooey.
Something salty; something sweet,
Hot beef jerky . . . what a treat!

Turn 'em to da left, turn 'em to da right,
Broil da chicken 'til it tastes out-a-sight!
Lift da wing and start to baste it,
It smells so ono, I can almost taste it!

Shoyu and sugar are the key ingredients,
Ooh . . . it's turning brown,
Pretty soon we'll be eating it!

Up from the depths of the ocean,
Bringing their towels and tanning lotion.
Having a beachin' day on the sand,
Even the Great White sports a tan.

Slice that fishcake thick, but neat,
To make some slippers for my feet!

KAMABOKO SLIPPERS

Strands of leis piled on top of me,
Are stacked so high, I can hardly see.
Auntie Pua brought pakalana,
From cousin Kimo . . . mokihana.
Carnation, maile, and lehua on top,
I look like a walking florist shop!

Order me one dozen bao,
For lunchtime, take-out, to eat right now.
Side order . . . rice cake and pepeao.

Good for eating on the run,
Roast pork and black sugar in steaming bun.
Bet you cannot eat just one!

Step right up to the best show in town!
Two days full of sights and sound.
It's February's big event.
Games of skill beneath the tent.

Hawaiian plate at the cafeteria.
Fast rides create mass hysteria.
Variety show by the theatrical troupe.
Heaping bowls of Portuguese bean soup.

Come for dinner and fill your bellies.
Take home jars of jams and jellies.
Bring your sistahs and your bruddahs.
Take out bags of malasadas.

Mister Squid, please pass that dish;
The one heaped with broiled butterfish.
Then with another arm that's free,
Please pass the plate of opihi.

Next, the limu and poki to kau kau,
Lomi salmon, pipikaula, and laulau.
Use your fingers . . . forget knife and fork,
We'll finish with kalua pork.

I'm in a pickle, decisions to make;
What type of side dish to add to my plate?

Kim chee goes well with my meal of kal bi.
Ume would do nicely in my musubi.

Mango and takuan taste great . . . guarantee.
After sweet Maui onion, no one will kiss me!

It's a tricky decision, more tough than you think.
Any pickle dish I choose goin' make my breath stink!

Side out! Bad call!
Geckos serve aloha ball.

A dig . . . a set,
A spike at the net!

Slam in your face!
Another ace!

The other guys stink!
We've skunked the skinks!

Sushi à la carte,
Choose your filling.
Tuna or crab,
Raw squid, if you're willing.

Clam or fish eggs sure sound nice,
Anything tastes good . . . wrapped in rice!

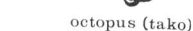

Honolulu Zoo inside a box.
Mynah birds and fighting cocks.
Real maninis on the loose.
Geckos and the sly mongoose.

Want fast food? See the Tako Belle.
With eight arms that can fly like hell.
Takes orders, serves, and cooks so well
Those mollusks on a taco shell.

Colorful kois fill the sky today,
To honor our boys.
It's the fifth of May.

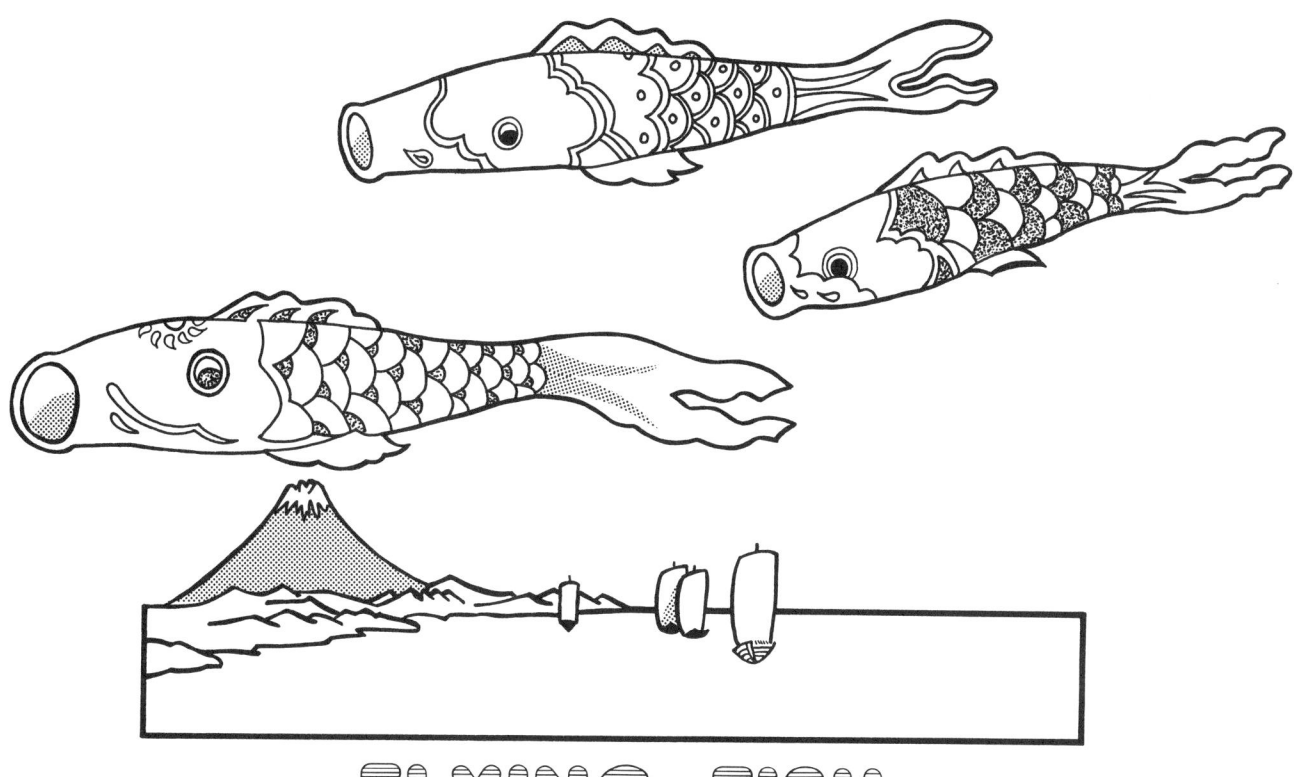

Jammin' and singin' at grandma's luau;
Too many beers for Uncle Keau!

In winter, Banzai Pipeline's ride
Is much like committing suicide.
Like a kamikaze with a death wish
I'm riding twenty feet above the fish.
The violent spray and frothing foam,
Make me wish I'd stayed at home!

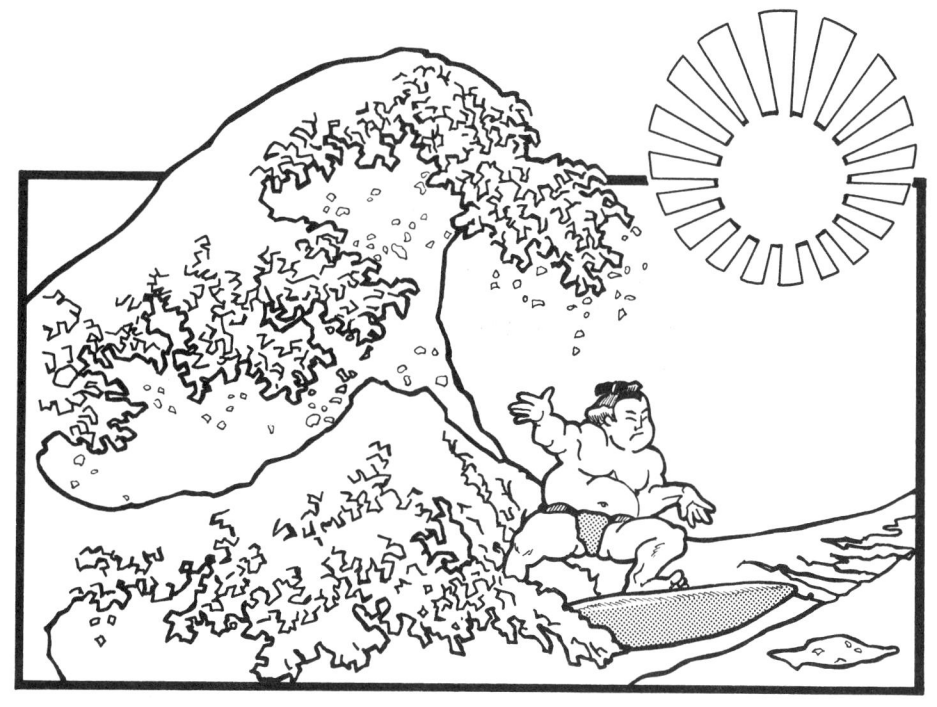

Lunch wagon's here!
The line forms to the rear.
The hardest thing is trying to decide . . .
Do I want tripe stew with rice on the side?
Or chicken adobo, or sweet-sour fish?
Or kal bi broiled ribs with a kim chee side dish?

LUNCH WAGON.. MEAL ON WHEELS

From the field, get and drag in,
One large ox with tail a waggin'.
Persuade the beast to sit with tail
Gently draped in water-filled pail.

Add peanuts, lotus root; then boil.
For spice, a touch of sesame seed oil.
A word of caution in making this stew . . .
Be sure to get the ox before he gets you!

Pass the Maui chips, my friend.
Here's some mochi crunch,
Manapua and cookies.
I'm too full for lunch!

TV's blaring; we're on the couch,
Semi-reclined.
Grinding snacks, local style,
Is our favorite pastime.

Waikiki Beach once was his turf,
Teaching tourists how to surf.
Part gigolo . . . a ladies' man,
Part lifeguard with chocolate tan.

Immortalized in local lore,
This hunk once ruled both surf and shore.
You'll hardly find him anymore,
He's gone the way of the dinosaur.

They're aptly named . . . the Sandwich Isles.
Our local foods of many styles
Laid end to end would stretch for miles.

Our Pacific home's a gathering place.
Like sandwiches of varied tastes,
We live together . . . every race.

ORDER BLANK

Please send me _____ copies of ISLAND STYLE @ $9.95 each*.

I am enclosing my check or money order for $ _____, payable to BESS PRESS.

_____
Name (Please print)

_____
Address

_____
City   State   Zip

*Price includes tax and handling charges. Allow 4-6 weeks for delivery.

BESS PRESS
P. O. BOX 22388
HONOLULU, HI 96823